A **TRUE** BOOK

National Military Park
Gettysburg

MOIRA ROSE DONOHUE

Children's Press®
An Imprint of Scholastic Inc.

Content Consultant

James Gramann, PhD
Professor Emeritus, Department of Recreation, Park and Tourism Sciences
Texas A&M University, College Station, Texas

Library of Congress Cataloging-in-Publication Data
Names: Donohue, Moira Rose, author. | Gramann, James H., consultant.
Title: Gettysburg / by Moira Rose Donohue ; content consultant, James Gramann, PhD, Professor
    Emeritus, Department of Recreation, Park and Tourism Sciences, Texas A&M University, College
    Station, Texas.
Description: New York, NY : Children's Press, [2019] | Series: A true book | Includes bibliographical
    references and index.
Identifiers: LCCN 2018032565| ISBN 9780531129326 (library binding) | ISBN 9780531135013 (pbk.)
Subjects: LCSH: Gettysburg, Battle of, Gettysburg, Pa., 1863—Juvenile literature. | Gettysburg
    National Military Park (Pa.)—Juvenile literature.
Classification: LCC E475.53 .D69 2019 | DDC 973.7/349—dc23
LC record available at https://lccn.loc.gov/2018032565

All rights reserved. Published in 2019 by Children's Press, an imprint of Scholastic Inc.
Printed in Heshan, China 62

SCHOLASTIC, CHILDREN'S PRESS, A TRUE BOOK™, and associated logos are trademarks and/or
registered trademarks of Scholastic Inc.

Scholastic Inc., 557 Broadway, New York, NY 10012

1 2 3 4 5 6 7 8 9 10 R 28 27 26 25 24 23 22 21 20 19

Front cover (main): A cannon in the field

Front cover (inset): Reenactors

Back cover: President Abraham
Lincoln at Gettysburg

Find the Truth!

Everything you are about to read is true *except* for one of the sentences on this page.

Which one is **TRUE**?

T or F   The Battle of Gettysburg was the deadliest battle ever fought in the United States.

T or F   The Confederates won the Battle of Gettysburg.

 Find the answers in this book.

Contents

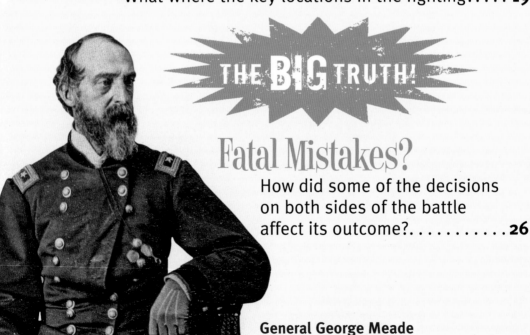

THE **BIG** TRUTH!

Fatal Mistakes?

**General George Meade
of the Union Army**

4

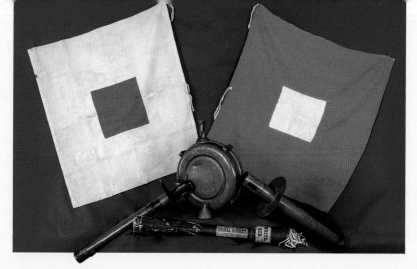

Square flags, torches with fuel, and rockets used for signaling

First Shot Marker

Nearly 630 cannons were used in the Battle of Gettysburg.

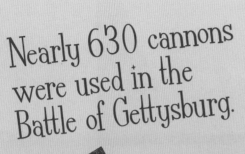

CHAPTER 1

Where History Happened

Gettysburg National Military Park

If you stand in Gettysburg National Military Park, listen closely for an echo of cannons booming. The Battle of Gettysburg took place here in southern Pennsylvania in 1863. It changed the course of the Civil War (1861–1865). More than 51,000 soldiers were wounded or died during the three-day battle. The battlefield is about 6,000 acres (2,428 hectares), just under half the size of Manhattan. It's a place to explore and to remember.

Historians know of only five surviving copies of President Lincoln's speech written in his own hand.

Addressing Gettysburg

Gettysburg is also famous because it's where President Abraham Lincoln made an unforgettable speech. On November 19, 1863, Lincoln spoke at the **dedication** of the cemetery at Gettysburg. Close to 20,000 people crowded around the stage to hear him. His speech, which became known as the Gettysburg Address, urged listeners to remember the soldiers who died there. You can see a monument to the Gettysburg Address in the park.

Forming Gettysburg

About 180 million years ago, **geological** activity thrust a 2,000-foot (610 meters) slab of rock into the Gettysburg region. Today, we call this slab the Gettysburg Sill. At the same time, two vertical rock formations called dikes were pushed into the area. These dikes raised land to form hills such as Little Round Top. They also created two parallel ridges: Cemetery Ridge and Seminary Ridge. These formations would play an important role in the Battle of Gettysburg.

Much of Gettysburg is rolling, rocky hills and valleys.

Creating the Park

After the battle, the governor of Pennsylvania purchased 17 acres (6.9 ha) on Cemetery Ridge, located on the battlefield. The land was used to bury the soldiers who had died. A few years later, the U.S. government took over the cemetery. Then in 1895, Congress made the battlefield a national military park. At the park, you can visit the cemetery and a museum that opened in 2008. You can also trace the footsteps of the soldiers who fought and died here.

A sign welcomes visitors to the park's Visitor Center.

National Park Service
U.S. Department of the Interior

Gettysburg
National Military Park
Visitor Center

National Park Fact File

A national park is land that is protected by the federal government. It is a place of importance to the United States because of its beauty, history, or value to scientists. The U.S. Congress creates a national park by passing a law. Here are some key facts about Gettysburg National Military Park.

Gettysburg National Military Park	
Location	Southern Pennsylvania
Year established	1895
Size	9.4 square miles (24.4 square kilometers)
Average number of visitors each year	More than 1 million
Number of monuments in the park	More than 1,300
Most popular place	Where Lincoln gave the Gettysburg Address
Notable attractions	Giant painting of Pickett's Charge, historical houses, battle sites

An estimated 750,000 to 850,000 people died in the Civil War. That's about 2 percent of the U.S. population at the time.

Union (in blue) and Confederate (in gray) troops fight in Georgia.

CHAPTER 2

A Civil War

Most wars are fights between two or more countries. A civil war is a fight between groups within a country. The Civil War was a clash between the Northern and Southern parts of the United States. The North was called the Union, and the South was known as the Confederacy. The Union soldiers wore blue uniforms. The Confederate uniform was gray. At the museum, you can see actual uniforms worn by soldiers in both armies.

Freeing the Slaves

Why were Americans fighting one another? In the 1800s, slavery was a common practice in the South. African people had been brought to this country against their will and sold as property to Southern farmers for centuries. Owners forced them to work long hours with no pay, no education, and no freedom. Slavery became an important part of the farming **economy** in the South. Then Abraham Lincoln was elected president in 1860. He had talked for many years against slavery.

Any children born to a slave parent on plantations, or elsewhere across the country, automatically became slaves themselves.

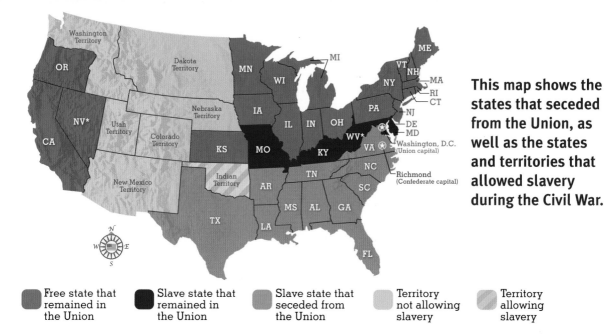

This map shows the states that seceded from the Union, as well as the states and territories that allowed slavery during the Civil War.

Free state that remained in the Union

Slave state that remained in the Union

Slave state that seceded from the Union

Territory not allowing slavery

Territory allowing slavery

* West Virginia and Nevada were admitted into the Union during the Civil War.

Southern states were upset with the new president's views. They announced that they were seceding from, or leaving, the United States. Lincoln and others in the Northern states believed that the country should stay united. They argued that under the U.S. Constitution, states did not have the right to secede. Before long, this disagreement turned into a war. Even territories, which were controlled by the United States but not yet states, were caught up in the fighting.

Friend Against Friend

In the Civil War, friends and even family members joined armies on opposite sides of the war. Some of these people even faced one another directly in battle. Imagine having to fight against your best friend. This happened among regular soldiers and high-ranking officers alike. The Battle of Gettysburg was no different.

Timeline of Civil War Milestones

1860

Abraham Lincoln is elected president. South Carolina becomes the first state to secede.

1863

The Union wins the Battle of Gettysburg. Lincoln delivers the Gettysburg Address.

1861

Several more Southern states secede. The first shots of the Civil War are fired at Fort Sumter in South Carolina.

At Gettysburg, Union general Winfield Scott Hancock fought against his best friend, Confederate general Lewis A. Armistead. Hancock was wounded during the battle, but Armistead was killed. As Armistead was dying, he asked Hancock's assistant to deliver his watch to his best friend. You can see a monument to this event at the park. It's called the Friend to Friend Masonic Memorial.

1872
The U.S. government takes over the cemetery at Gettysburg.

1895
U.S. Congress makes the Gettysburg battlefield a national military park.

1865
The Union wins the Civil War.

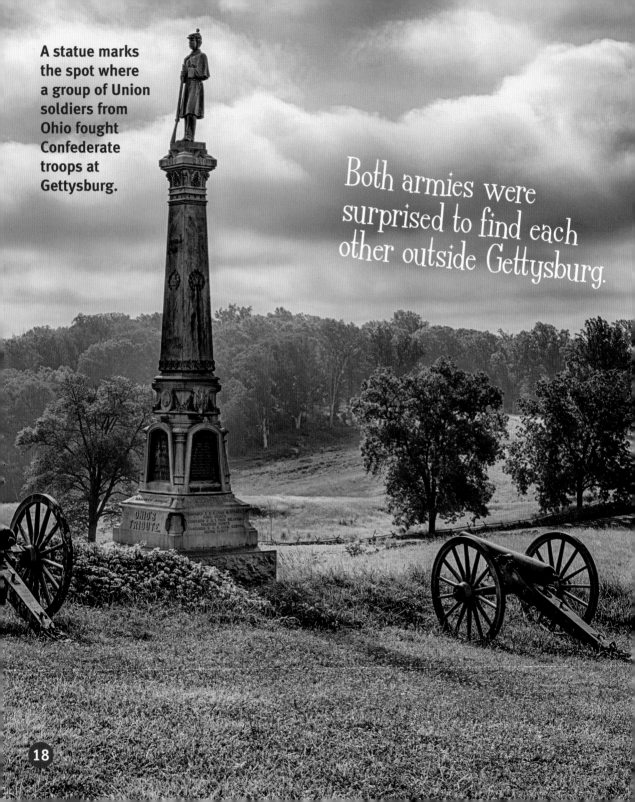

A statue marks the spot where a group of Union soldiers from Ohio fought Confederate troops at Gettysburg.

Both armies were surprised to find each other outside Gettysburg.

Three Days of Battle

General Robert E. Lee commanded the Confederate army. After several victories in the South, Lee set out to invade the North with about 75,000 soldiers. On July 1, 1863, he unexpectedly ran into the Union army outside Gettysburg, Pennsylvania. Roughly 90,000 Union troops were there. Violence erupted, and the Battle of Gettysburg began.

The Union had more troops, but the Confederates forced them back. The Union soldiers scrambled to the high ground of Cemetery Ridge.

Rocky Ridges

The Confederate army marched to the top of the nearby Seminary Ridge, just opposite the Union troops. Looking across an open field, the Confederates could see the Union soldiers. You can climb up Seminary Ridge today and gaze across the same field.

During the night, General George Meade arrived to take charge of the Union army. The next afternoon, on the second day of the battle, the Confederates attacked both ends of the Union line.

Confederate soldiers, held as prisoners after the battle, rest against a fence on Seminary Ridge.

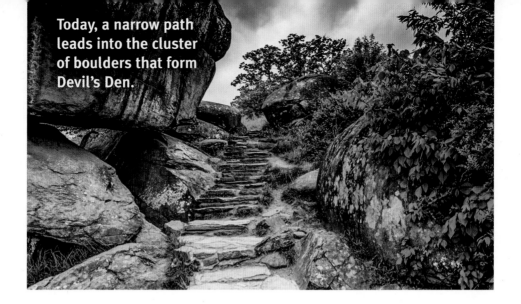
Today, a narrow path leads into the cluster of boulders that form Devil's Den.

Devil's Den

Cannons boomed and filled the air with smoke. As the haze cleared, Union soldiers on the south end of the line came face-to-face with Confederate soldiers. The Confederates were advancing through the Wheatfield and the Peach Orchard.

Some Union soldiers scrambled up into Devil's Den, but Confederates followed. Devil's Den is a cluster of granite boulders. Granite is a type of igneous rock, which is made of hardened molten rock called magma.

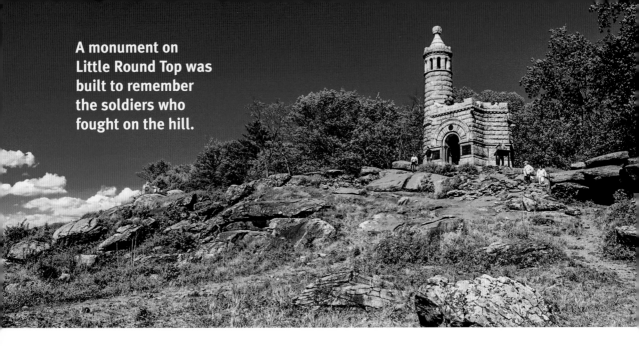

A monument on Little Round Top was built to remember the soldiers who fought on the hill.

Little Round Top

Right behind Devil's Den is a 650-foot (198 m) hill called Little Round Top. Union general Gouverneur K. Warren ordered a group of soldiers to race up the unprotected hill and hold it. They soon began to run out of ammunition, but they refused to **surrender**. They attached sharp **bayonets** to their guns and fought hand to hand. The brave soldiers held the hill. Today, Little Round Top is one of the most visited places in the park.

Pickett's Charge

On July 3, the third day of fighting, General Lee ordered an attack on the middle of the Union line on Cemetery Ridge. General George Pickett from Virginia led the attack. His soldiers were enthusiastic, but they didn't have much battle experience. With loud battle cries, they charged ahead, across the open field and straight into enemy fire.

About 15,000 Confederate soldiers took part in Pickett's Charge.

Confederate Retreat

Many men on both sides died. But at the end of the day, the Union fought the Confederates back. Today, the High Water Mark monument shows the farthest point Pickett's men reached.

The failure of Pickett's Charge turned the battle against the Confederates. On July 5, they began their **retreat** south. President Lincoln wanted General Meade to follow and fight them immediately, but Meade waited. Soon, it was too late to catch the Confederates.

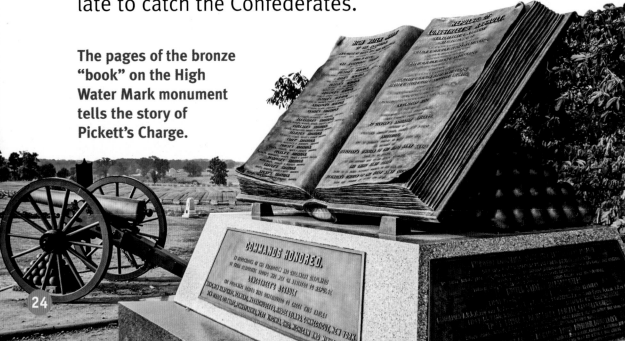

The pages of the bronze "book" on the High Water Mark monument tells the story of Pickett's Charge.

A 360° Battle View

Before movies or television, people relied on artists to visually record history. Some artists, such as Paul Philippoteaux, painted **cycloramas**. These huge paintings completely surround the viewer. Philippoteaux painted one of Pickett's Charge. It first went on display in 1883. It's as tall as a four-story building, and if laid flat it would be longer than a football field. The painting, now in the park's Visitor Center, has survived fire and water. If you stand in the middle of it, you may feel like you're part of the battle.

Fatal Mistakes?

Strategy is an important part of winning a war. To make a decision in battle, generals and other leaders study a situation and try to guess the enemy's next move. It is not always easy, and sometimes leaders make the wrong choice. Read about two controversial decisions that decided the battle and how the war ended.

General George Meade
(Union Army)

General Robert E. Lee
(Confederate Army)

July 3, Morning
After two days of fighting at Gettysburg, General Lee was winning. He believed the Union army was spread thin in the middle of their line. So he ordered Pickett to charge that area.

July 3, Afternoon
The Union troops were located high on Cemetery Ridge. Height is a serious advantage. It is easier to fight from above than from below. The Union showered Pickett's men with bullets. The Confederates fell back.

July 5
Both sides were exhausted after the battle and rested on July 4. The next day, the Confederates began their retreat. Rain slowed them down. Instead of immediately following the Confederates, General Meade chose to wait. The war continued on for another two years after that.

Battle of Gettysburg
Day 3: July 3, 1863
- Union Troops
- Confederate Troops

0   1/2   1
Miles

Had General Lee tried a different strategy, could the Confederates have won the battle or even the war?

Should General Meade have followed the retreating Confederates immediately, while the enemy was weakened by battle? If he had, could Meade have forced the Confederacy to surrender then, shortening the war by as much as two years?

The National Park Service takes care of 14 national cemeteries, including the one at Gettysburg.

Flags decorate the Soldiers' National Cemetery at Gettysburg.

The Gettysburg Address

The Battle of Gettysburg may have been the most important battle in the Civil War. Though Lee had many victories beforehand, Gettysburg turned the tide of the war toward the Union. In 1865, the Union won.

About 7,000 soldiers died at Gettysburg. It remains the deadliest battle ever fought in the United States. At the park, you can visit the cemetery where 3,500 Union soldiers, along with **veterans** from more recent wars, are buried.

The bedroom where President Lincoln stayed before delivering the Gettysburg Address has been preserved to look as it did in 1863.

Words to Remember

The cemetery at Gettysburg was opened not long after the battle, and long before the war was over. President Lincoln rode the train from Washington, D.C., the night before the Gettysburg Address in November 1863. Today, you can visit the David Wills House where Lincoln slept the night he arrived. The route he took on horseback to the cemetery the next morning is also marked.

Equipment of the Day

At the time of the Civil War, phones and radios didn't exist. Messages were sent using signals from rockets, torches, or flags. There were no water bottles either. Soldiers carried water in canteens.

Some things don't change. Like the soldiers of today, both sides used field glasses to watch the enemy!

Canteen

Signal flag

Signal flag

Fuel for torches

Torch

Torch

Field glasses

Rocket

"Of the People"

The speech Lincoln gave at the dedication was about 270 words long and took only two minutes to deliver. He stated in his speech that people would not remember his words, though they would remember the battle. But people do remember his words. He insisted that we preserve our government, established "of the people, by the people, and for the people." Listen closely and perhaps you will hear an echo of these words today.

The Gettysburg Address was short compared to other speeches of the time, which could last hours.

This is one of only two possible photographs of President Lincoln at the Gettysburg cemetery dedication.

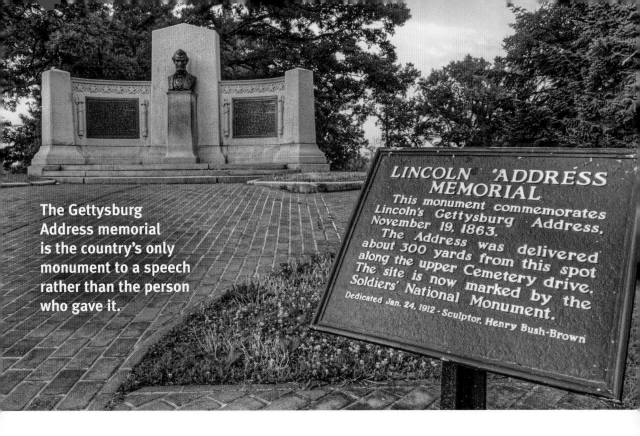

The Gettysburg Address memorial is the country's only monument to a speech rather than the person who gave it.

LINCOLN 'ADDRESS MEMORIAL
This monument commemorates Lincoln's Gettysburg Address, November 19, 1863.
The Address was delivered about 300 yards from this spot along the upper Cemetery drive. The site is now marked by the Soldiers' National Monument.
Dedicated Jan. 24, 1912 - Sculptor, Henry Bush-Brown

A memorial stands in the park in honor of Lincoln's famous speech. In the center is a sculpture of Lincoln's head and shoulders. On one side is his Gettysburg Address. On the other are the words of the president's official invitation to the dedication. This memorial does not mark the place where Lincoln stood as he spoke. He actually spoke his famous words in the cemetery nearby.

Tourists on Segway scooters travel through Gettysburg National Military Park.

CHAPTER 5

Gettysburg Today

Millions of people travel to Gettysburg National Military Park each year. If you visit, it's a good idea to start at the Museum and Visitor Center. Then you can tour the park by car, bus, Segway scooter, bicycle, or foot. Some people even experience Gettysburg on horseback. The most common question people ask is, "Where did Lincoln deliver the Gettysburg Address?"

 Guided tours through Gettysburg can last from 2 hours to a full day.

Before the battle started, soldiers might have heard the musical song of the black-throated blue warbler.

Preserving History

You might see animals such as white-tailed deer, spotted turtles, and red foxes at the park. If you look up, you may spy a black-throated blue warbler in the trees. Look for plants such as skunk cabbage and even peach trees bearing fruit. The park rangers are working to bring back and protect these and other plants and animals that lived in the area during the battle.

Witness Trees

A few of the park's oak trees have been around since before the battle in 1863. These aged oaks are called witness trees. Historians know they were alive at the time of the battle because the trees are marked with bullet holes!

Unfortunately, most of the witness trees have died or have been cut down because of disease or damage. Before cutting a tree down, rangers save the section of it that shows where gunfire hit.

Reliving History

In the spring and summer, park rangers give living history demonstrations. People dress in costumes and demonstrate how to use tools from the battle. They even fire some of the 400 old cannons located in the park.

The National Park Service and the Gettysburg Foundation preserve the grounds and the monuments. You can volunteer to help. Volunteers paint fences and may even clean a cannon!

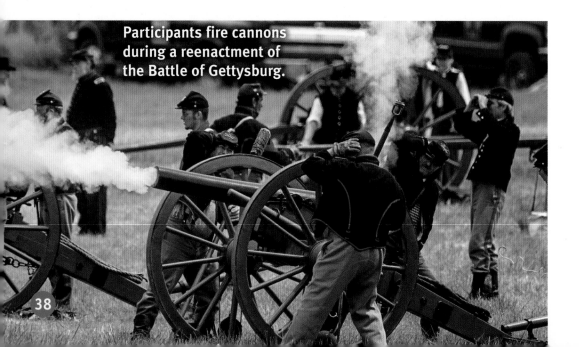

Participants fire cannons during a reenactment of the Battle of Gettysburg.

Never Forget

Most visitors stop to see the various monuments that honor the generals and armies from across the country. They visit memorials to the soldiers who died and markers that **commemorate** important moments in the battle. Like many people, you might want to stand on Little Round Top or find the spot where Lincoln gave his famous speech. One thing is for certain—if you visit Gettysburg National Military Park, you will never forget it. ★

People sometimes leave coins or other objects on the headstones of soldiers to show that someone who cared has visited.

Be a Monument Tracker!

If you're ever in Gettysburg National Military Park, keep an eye out for these monuments. These markers can help you remember important moments in the battle.

Eternal Light Peace Memorial

Built in 1938 on the 75th anniversary of the battle, this monument honors Gettysburg veterans.

Women's Memorial

This statue recognizes the women who helped and suffered during the battle.

First Shot Marker

The pillar here marks where Union officer Marcellus Jones fired what most people agree was the battle's first shot.

Spangler's Spring

Here, soldiers from both sides refilled their canteens with water bubbling up from the ground.

John Burns Memorial

This statue honors John Burns, a 69-year-old local man who joined the fighting alongside the Union army during the battle.

State of Pennsylvania Monument

The park's largest memorial, this structure honors Pennsylvania's soldiers who fought in the battle.

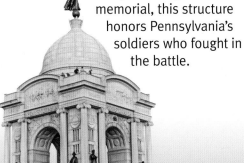

Map Mystery

In a cluster of trees, called a copse, sits a memorial that looks like a book. There are cannons on either side. What is this memorial called? Follow the directions below to find the answer.

Directions

1. Start at the Peach Orchard. Confederate soldiers crossed this spot on the second day of fighting.

2. Travel south across the Wheatfield to Devil's Den.

3. Head east and hike up Little Round Top.

4. Now walk north along Cemetery Ridge, where the Union line stood. Almost there!

5. Stop at Meades' Headquarters, just before you reach the Soldiers' National Cemetery. Look west. This is as far as Pickett and his men got.

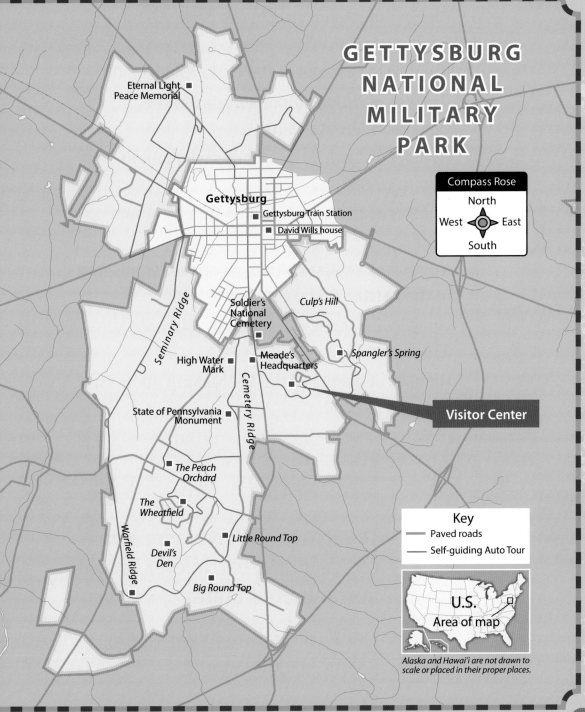

GETTYSBURG NATIONAL MILITARY PARK

Compass Rose

North
West — East
South

Eternal Light
Peace Memorial ■

Gettysburg

Gettysburg Train Station ■

■ David Wills house

Seminary Ridge

Soldier's
National
Cemetery ■

Culp's Hill

High Water
Mark ■

Meade's ■
Headquarters

■ *Spangler's Spring*

Cemetery Ridge

State of Pennsylvania ■
Monument

Visitor Center

■ *The Peach
Orchard*

*The
Wheatfield*

Warfield Ridge

■ *Little Round Top*

■ *Devil's
Den*

■ *Big Round Top*

Key
━━ Paved roads
── Self-guiding Auto Tour

U.S.
Area of map

*Alaska and Hawai'i are not drawn to
scale or placed in their proper places.*

True Statistics

Number of monuments in the park: About 1,320

Number of cannons in the park: About 400

Number of Union soldiers buried in the cemetery: About 3,500

Number of Confederate troops who fought: About 75,000

Number of Union troops who fought: About 90,000

Number of soldiers killed, wounded, or missing in the battle: Approximately 51,000

Length of Lincoln's Gettysburg Address: About 270 words

Number of people at the Gettysburg Address: Roughly 20,000

Did you find the truth?

T The Battle of Gettysburg was the deadliest battle ever fought in the United States.

F The Confederates won the Battle of Gettysburg.